BEST OF THE SUPER BOWL

STUNNING SUPER BOWL MOMENTS

BY DAVID J. CLARKE

SportsZone

An Imprint of Abdo Publishing
abdobooks.com

abdobooks.com

Published by Abdo Publishing, a division of ABDO, PO Box 398166, Minneapolis, Minnesota 55439.

Printed in the United States of America, North Mankato, Minnesota.
102024
012025

THIS BOOK CONTAINS RECYCLED MATERIALS

Cover Photo: Focus on Sport/Getty Images (left); Theo Wargo/Getty Images Sport/Getty Images (center); Focus on Sport/Getty Images Sport/Getty Images (right)
Interior Photos: Cooper Neill/AP Images, 4; Focus On Sport/Getty Images, 6, 22; Al Messerschmidt/AP Images, 9; Bettmann/Getty Images, 10; Doug Benc/Getty Images Sport/Getty Images, 13; Smiley N. Pool/Houston Chronicle/Hearst Newspapers/Getty Images, 14; Tony Tomsic/AP Images, 16; Focus On Sport/Getty Images Sport/Getty Images, 19, 37; Aaron M. Sprecher/Icon Sport Media/Icon Sportswire/Getty Images, 21; Gin Ellis/Getty Images Sport/Getty Images, 25; Wally McNamee/Corbis Historical/Getty Images, 26; Icon Sportswire/Getty Images, 27; Rich Pilling/Diamond Images/Getty Images, 29; G. N. Lowrance/NFLPhotoLibrary/Getty Images Sport/Getty Images, 31; Rich Graessle/Icon Sportswire/Getty Images, 33; Diamond Images/Getty Images, 34–35; George Rose/Getty Images Sport/Getty Images, 39; Jeff Kravitz/FilmMagic Inc./Getty Images, 41; Rob Tringali/SportsChrome/Getty Images, 43; Allen Kee/Getty Images Sport/Getty Images, 44; Frank Micelotta/Getty Images Entertainment/Getty Images, 45

Editor: Charlie Beattie
Series Designer: Jake Slavik

Library of Congress Control Number: 2024938340

Publisher's Cataloging-in-Publication Data

Names: Clarke, David J., author.
Title: Stunning Super Bowl moments / by David J. Clarke
Description: Minneapolis, Minnesota: ABDO Publishing, 2025 | Series: Best of the Super Bowl | Includes online resources and index.
Identifiers: ISBN 9781098295424 (lib. bdg.) | ISBN 9798384916420 (ebook)
Subjects: LCSH: Super Bowl--Records--Juvenile literature. | American football--Juvenile literature. | National Football League--Juvenile literature. | Football--United States--History--Juvenile literature.
Classification: DDC 796.332648--dc23

TABLE OF CONTENTS

15
15
Wilson

CHAPTER ONE

STUNNING OFFENSIVE PLAYS

Kansas City Chiefs quarterback Patrick Mahomes came into Super Bowl LVII in February 2023 nursing an ankle injury. He hurt it again midway through the game after a hard tackle. Yet, late in the fourth quarter the Chiefs were tied 35–35 with the Philadelphia Eagles. Kansas City needed a big play. On first-and-10 from the Eagles' 43-yard line, Mahomes was flushed from the pocket by the Eagles' pass rush. He broke free and managed to hobble 26 yards before he was caught. Mahomes's tough run set up the game-winning field goal. It was just the latest in a long line of great offensive plays.

Four decades earlier, another tough quarterback led the Pittsburgh Steelers. At the time, the National Football League (NFL)

Patrick Mahomes grimaces as he hobbles off the field after reinjuring his ankle in the first half of Super Bowl LVII in February 2023.

Terry Bradshaw (12) stood up against a fierce pass rush for the entire game in Super Bowl X after the 1975 season.

didn't have many rules to protect quarterbacks. They had to make plays while fierce linemen did whatever they could to pummel them. Terry Bradshaw excelled in these conditions at Super Bowl X after the 1975 season. With just under four minutes left in the game, the Steelers held a 15–10 lead over the Dallas Cowboys. From his own 36-yard line, Bradshaw dropped back to pass. He escaped the Dallas rush and heaved a long bomb downfield. It dropped into the waiting arms of receiver Lynn Swann, who raced for a touchdown.

The pass traveled 60 yards in the air. And while Bradshaw saw it go up, he missed the ball coming down. Just after he released the pass, Dallas lineman Larry Cole's helmet slammed into Bradshaw's chin. The Steelers' quarterback was knocked from the game. But it was not before he had delivered what NFL Films later called the greatest throw in league history.

Two decades after Bradshaw withstood the punishment coming his way, Denver Broncos quarterback John Elway leaned into it. Elway entered Super Bowl XXXII in January 1998 as a three-time loser in the game. At 37 years old, he was running out of chances. But with under two minutes left in the third quarter against the Green Bay Packers, Elway showed the world just how badly he wanted to win a title.

The teams were tied 17–17. On third down from the Green Bay 12-yard line, Elway scrambled to his right. With his receivers covered, his only choice was to run. The veteran quarterback took off and was met by three defenders at the 5-yard line. Instead of sliding down to avoid contact, Elway leaped headlong into all three players, who spun him around in the air. Elway landed with a thud, but he had picked up the first down.

Elway popped up and threw a celebratory fist in the air. His "helicopter" play set up a Denver touchdown. The Broncos went on to win the first of back-to-back titles, 31–24.

RUNNING FOR GLORY

Washington head coach Joe Gibbs had a big problem early in the fourth quarter of Super Bowl XVII on January 30, 1983. His team trailed the Miami Dolphins 17–13 with just over 10 minutes to play. Now Washington faced fourth-and-1 at the Miami 43-yard line. But Gibbs had a big solution to his big problem—6-foot, 2-inch, 230-pound running back John Riggins.

Gibbs dialed up a play called "70 chip." Riggins, nicknamed "Diesel" for his powerful runs, got the ball while running left. The Washington offensive line opened a big hole for him. Only Miami cornerback Don McNeal stood in the way. Riggins outweighed McNeal by 40 pounds and shrugged the cornerback off easily. From there, Diesel raced into the end zone for the go-ahead score. Washington won the game 27–17. Riggins was named the game's Most Valuable Player (MVP).

A year later, Washington was back in the Super Bowl. This time the team was on the wrong end of a huge run. While Riggins rushed with power, the Los Angeles Raiders' Marcus Allen was a lean, graceful runner. And on one third-quarter play, he made NFL history by going off script.

Super Bowl XVIII was already a blowout. The Raiders led 28–9 when Allen got the ball at the Los Angeles 26-yard line. He ran to the left, but found the way blocked by several defenders. So Allen stopped and reversed. Then he spotted a hole up the middle and

John Riggins's 43-yard touchdown in Super Bowl XVII on January 30, 1983, was the longest run he had that year.

Marcus Allen's 74-yard run was a Super Bowl record until 2006.

burst through it. Despite coming close to nearly every Washington defender, Allen was barely touched on his way to a then–Super Bowl record 74-yard rushing score. It was the signature moment of a 38–9 romp for Los Angeles.

CLUTCH CATCHES

Most football fans had not heard of New York Giants receiver David Tyree entering Super Bowl XLII in February 2008. He caught only four passes during the regular season. But by the end of the game, he was the talk of the football world.

Few gave the Giants a chance to win against the undefeated New England Patriots. But with under two minutes to go, New York had the ball and trailed only 14–10. On third-and-5 from the Giants 44, New York quarterback Eli Manning dropped back to pass. Patriots defenders immediately swarmed him. Manning somehow wriggled away and heaved a desperate pass down the middle of the field.

Tyree was waiting for it. So was hard-hitting New England safety Rodney Harrison. Both players leaped for the ball. Tyree grabbed it above his head. With Harrison trying to rip it out, the Giants receiver held tight. The ball stayed pinned to his helmet as both players slammed to the turf.

Tyree had held on for a 32-yard catch. Four plays later, Manning tossed the game-winning touchdown to Plaxico Burress. The Patriots' dream of becoming just the second undefeated Super Bowl champion was wiped out by the "helmet catch" that made the unknown Tyree an instant legend.

MANNING TO MANNINGHAM

Four years after David Tyree's incredible helmet catch, the Giants faced the Patriots again in Super Bowl XLVI. Once again, New York was the underdog. Down 17–15 with under three minutes to go, the Giants took over at their own 12-yard line. On the first play, Eli Manning tossed a ball down the left sideline into double coverage. Receiver Mario Manningham made a fingertip grab for a 38-yard gain. The Giants eventually scored to upset New England again.

A year after Tyree's catch, the Steelers and Arizona Cardinals played another tight Super Bowl game in Tampa, Florida. The Cardinals had scored 16 points in the fourth quarter to rally for a 23–20 lead. Steelers quarterback Ben Roethlisberger then guided his team down the field and set up second-and-goal from the 6-yard line with under a minute to play. The quarterback scanned the field for an open receiver and didn't find one. Instead, he tried to rifle a pass to the back right corner of the end zone.

Steelers receiver Santonio Holmes was in that corner. But he was hardly open. Three Cardinals defenders surrounded him. Somehow, Roethlisberger managed to get his pass over all three defenders. Holmes stretched for it and made a fingertip grab. He then managed to come down with his toes barely inbounds.

Pittsburgh's defense stopped the Cardinals on the next drive. The Steelers secured their sixth Super Bowl title. It was all thanks to Holmes's "Tampa Toe Tap" in the corner of the end zone.

Santonio Holmes stretches for his game-winning touchdown catch in Super Bowl XLIII on February 1, 2009.

Rams
LYLE

CHAPTER TWO

STUNNING DEFENSIVE PLAYS

The 1999 St. Louis Rams were known for their high-flying offense. Dubbed the "Greatest Show on Turf," St. Louis set an NFL scoring record on its way to Super Bowl XXXIV. But it was a defensive play that secured a thrilling win on Super Sunday against the Tennessee Titans.

St. Louis led 23–16 with just seconds remaining when Tennessee quarterback Steve McNair dropped back to throw. He rifled a pass to receiver Kevin Dyson over the middle. Dyson was immediately hit by Rams linebacker Mike Jones. As the Titans receiver struggled and stretched toward the goal line, Jones hung on. As Dyson fell, he reached as far as he could. But his knee hit the turf with the ball still one yard short of the end zone as the clock ran out.

Mike Jones, *left*, celebrates after his game-saving tackle on the final play of Super Bowl XXXIV in January 2000.

Jones's tackle was just one of many amazing defensive plays in Super Bowl history. In January 1982, the San Francisco 49ers were facing the Cincinnati Bengals in Super Bowl XVI. San Francisco held a 20–7 lead in the third quarter. But the Bengals had already scored once in the second half, and the game's momentum was shifting. San Francisco needed a big stop.

Lineman Archie Reese (78) smothers the top of the pile after the San Francisco 49ers stopped the Cincinnati Bengals in Super Bowl XVI on January 24, 1982.

The Bengals had 249-pound fullback Pete Johnson, who rumbled to the 1-yard line on first down. Cincinnati coach Forrest Gregg turned to Johnson on second down again. This time, San Francisco linebacker Jack "Hacksaw" Reynolds slammed into the big running back. Johnson lost a yard.

On third down, Gregg's Bengals tried a pass play. Quarterback Ken Anderson swung a pass to running back Charles Alexander in the right flat. Alexander was inches from the goal line when he caught the ball. But he was immediately flattened by San Francisco linebacker Dan Bunz to set up fourth down.

After a timeout, the Bengals decided to go for it. Johnson ran right and dove straight into a wall of 49ers, led by Reynolds. The Bengals turned the ball over on downs.

Cincinnati still mounted a late comeback, but San Francisco held on to

THEISMANN PLAYS DEFENSE

Joe Theismann was a star quarterback for Washington in the 1970s and 1980s. But some quick thinking led to a game-saving defensive play in Super Bowl XVII. Trying to throw from his own 18-yard line late in the third quarter, Theismann's pass was batted in the air by Miami Dolphins lineman Kim Bokamper. Both players scrambled for it as it sailed back toward the Washington end zone. Theismann got there just in time to bat it away and prevent an interception and a touchdown. The score was 17–13 Miami at the time. Washington eventually won 27–17.

win its first Super Bowl 26–21. The 49ers would win four more titles in the next 14 years, mostly behind a powerful offense. But it was the San Francisco defense that helped launch a dynasty.

BUTLER'S BIG PLAY

In Super Bowl XLIX in February 2015, two powerhouse teams met at the goal line. The Seattle Seahawks were the defending champions. But the New England Patriots were the best team of the 2000s. A thrilling Super Bowl matchup between the two came down to a second-and-goal play for the Seahawks with 26 seconds left.

Seattle brought the ball to the Patriots 1-yard line. With the Seahawks trailing 28–24, everyone assumed they would go to powerful running back Marshawn Lynch. The 5-foot-11, 215-pound Lynch was known as one of the toughest runners in the league. His "beast mode" runs were a big part of Seattle's success.

Instead, Seattle head coach Pete Carroll decided to pass. Quarterback Russell Wilson took a quick drop and gunned a ball over the middle to receiver Ricardo Lockette. Patriots cornerback Malcolm Butler stepped in and intercepted the throw, sealing the win for New England.

Afterward, the football world expressed shock at Carroll's decision. Seahawks fans were left to wonder what might have been. As it was, the Patriots won their first Super Bowl in 10 years and began a new dynasty. They had won two more Super Bowls by the

Malcolm Butler, *left*, bounces off Seattle receiver Ricardo Lockette after making his game-winning interception against the Seahawks.

end of the 2018 season. Carroll left the Seahawks in 2024 without guiding his team to the big game again.

PICK SIXES

James Harrison was an intimidating presence on the Pittsburgh Steelers defense leading up to Super Bowl XLIII in February 2009. The linebacker was known for his punishing hits. He had been the American Football Conference (AFC) Defensive Player of the Year that season. However, he was not known for his speed.

On the final play of the first half against the Arizona Cardinals, Pittsburgh held a 10–7 lead. But the Cardinals had the ball at the Steelers' 2. Harrison dropped into coverage and intercepted Kurt Warner's pass at the goal line. He then began a lumbering 100-yard dash to the opposite end zone. Harrison was almost caught multiple times by chasing Cardinals. At one point, he had to hurdle a teammate blocking for him. Harrison barely had enough left to get into the end zone as Arizona wide receiver Larry Fitzgerald clung to his back.

Exhausted from hauling his 242-pound frame the length of the field, Harrison needed the team trainer's help to get up. It was the only pick six of the superstar's career. It was also the longest defensive play in Super Bowl history.

A year later, the New Orleans Saints and Indianapolis Colts squared off in Super Bowl XLIV. In a tight game, the Saints took a 24–17 lead with 5:42 left. But that was plenty of time for Colts quarterback Peyton Manning. The superstar moved Indianapolis to the New Orleans 31-yard line with just over three minutes remaining.

All game, Saints corner Tracy Porter had been matched up with Colts star receiver Reggie Wayne. When Wayne cut to the middle of the field this time, Porter jumped in front of him and snagged Manning's pass at the 26-yard line. The 23-year-old Porter sped past the chasing Manning and into the open field. He raced the distance to seal New Orleans' first Super Bowl championship.

Tracy Porter points to the scoreboard as he sprints to the end zone to seal New Orleans' win in Super Bowl XLIV after the 2009 season.

CHAPTER THREE

BLOOPERS, MISTAKES, AND TRICK PLAYS

Garo Yepremian grew up on the tiny island of Cyprus in the Mediterranean Sea. Soccer was his sport of choice, and Yepremian knew little of American football. A star soccer player, he came to the United States to play that sport at Indiana University. He only tried football after his brother suggested Garo might be good at it.

Yepremian became an excellent NFL kicker. His Miami Dolphins reached the Super Bowl VII after the 1972 season. He had already kicked two extra points, helping the team to a 14–0 lead over Washington. With just over two minutes remaining, Yepremian lined up a 42-yard field goal attempt to put the game away. The Dolphins were on their way to a 17–0 season, the first perfect year in

Garo Yepremian loads up to attempt his ill-fated pass in Super Bowl VII after the 1972 season.

NFL history. But Yepremian's kick was blocked, and it only got worse from there. He scrambled to pick up the ball, and then tried to throw a pass. The ball bobbled comically off his hand, bounced off his other arm, and flopped straight into the hands of Washington's Mike Bass. The Washington defender raced 49 yards for a touchdown.

In the end, Yepremian's gaffe didn't matter. The Dolphins won 14–7 to complete their perfect season. Yepremian won the Super Bowl again the next year. But football fans have never forgotten his ill-fated "pass."

EARLY CELEBRATION

Super Bowl XXVII was one of the all-time blowouts. Dallas routed the Buffalo Bills 52–17. But that scoreline could have been even worse for Buffalo if not for a huge mistake from Cowboys defensive tackle Leon Lett.

Lett was one of the stars of Dallas' defense. And with 4:54 left in the game, he had a chance to put an exclamation point on the Cowboys' huge win. On fourth-and-5 from the Dallas 31-yard line, Bills quarterback Frank Reich dropped back to pass. Cowboys defensive end Jim Jeffcoat drilled him. The ball came loose and popped right into Lett's arms. The 6-foot, 6-inch lineman began rumbling toward the far end zone, and no one was in his way.

Thinking he was in the clear, Lett started to celebrate at the Buffalo 10-yard line. He held the ball down by his waist. But Lett

Don Beebe, *left*, chases down Leon Lett in Super Bowl XXVII in January 1993.

didn't see that Bills wide receiver Don Beebe had come streaking down the sideline. Beebe chopped the ball from Lett's hand, and it bounced into the end zone and out of bounds. Instead of a touchdown, it was a touchback, and the Bills kept the ball. While Lett never lived down his infamous play, many chose to praise Beebe for his hustle despite the lopsided score.

SUPER MISTAKES

Less than three minutes remained in the third quarter of Super Bowl XIII on January 21, 1979. The Dallas Cowboys were down 21–14

Jackie Smith caught 480 passes in his 16 NFL seasons, but his Super Bowl drop haunted him for years.

against the Pittsburgh Steelers. Dallas faced a third-and-3 from the Pittsburgh 10-yard line. As quarterback Roger Staubach dropped back to pass, he spotted veteran tight end Jackie Smith wide open in the end zone. Smith sank to his knees to catch Staubach's low pass, only for the ball to bounce off his chest and onto the turf.

As the 38-year-old Smith pounded the end zone grass in anger, Dallas radio announcer Verne Lundquist summed up the moment perfectly: "Bless his heart," said Lundquist. "He's got to be the sickest man in America." Though Dallas kicked a field goal on the next play, that wasn't enough. Pittsburgh won 35–31. Had Smith caught the touchdown pass, those additional four points would have made up the difference.

Twelve years after Smith's drop, the New York Giants and Buffalo Bills battled in Super Bowl XXV after the 1990 season. With eight seconds left, a Buffalo drive stalled at the New York 29. With Buffalo down 20–19, kicker Scott Norwood came on for a 47-yard field goal attempt to win the game.

Norwood was 20-for-29 on field goal attempts during the 1990 season. He made 5-of-7 in the playoffs. But Super Bowl XXV was being played on

THURMAN THOMAS'S HELMET

The Buffalo Bills had high hopes before Super Bowl XXVI. They had come within a point of victory over the New York Giants the year before. And with Buffalo's high-powered offense set to take the field to open the game against Washington, Bills fans were hopeful for a hot start. But the team had to take its first snap without star running back Thurman Thomas. He had misplaced his helmet on the sideline. The Bills' equipment staff eventually found it. Thomas missed only two plays, but the confusion set the tone for Buffalo's ugly 37–24 loss.

a grass field. At that point, Norwood had never kicked a field goal longer than 41 yards on grass. Norwood stepped up and blasted the ball, and then watched as it drifted wide of the right upright. The Giants held on to win.

Super Bowl XXV was the first of four straight that the Bills would play in. They lost all four. But while the other three were lopsided games, "wide right" is still remembered as the best chance Buffalo had. Norwood played one more season for the Bills, and he never lived down his missed kick.

THE FRIDGE

Defensive tackle William "the Refrigerator" Perry was a big man for the 1985 Chicago Bears. At the time, the average NFL lineman weighed around 270 pounds. Perry's 6-foot, 2-inch, 335-pound frame made him a giant. While on offense in goal-line situations, Bears head coach Mike Ditka frequently lined Perry up in the backfield on offense to block for the team's legendary running back, Walter Payton. But the Fridge had also scored two touchdowns during the 1985 regular season.

The Bears were already routing the New England Patriots in Super Bowl XX when Chicago lined up at the New England 1-yard line late in the third quarter. Perry set up next to Payton in the backfield. The crowd inside New Orleans' Superdome erupted when quarterback Jim McMahon handed Perry the ball. Sure enough, Perry steamrolled

William "Refrigerator" Perry, *center*, blasts his way into the end zone to score in Super Bowl XX on January 26, 1986.

a defender as he lumbered into the end zone. It was the most memorable moment of a dominant 46–10 Chicago victory.

While it was exciting at the time, many fans wished that Ditka had called a play for Payton, who was the Bears' most popular player. It was the superstar's 12th year in the league, but his only Super Bowl appearance. Instead, Payton finished the game without scoring. Later, Ditka said that snubbing Payton was the biggest mistake of his coaching career.

TRICKY IN PITTSBURGH

With just under 11 minutes to play in Super Bowl XL on February 5, 2006, the Steelers picked off a pass from Seattle Seahawks quarterback Matt Hasselbeck. Pittsburgh held a slim 14–10 lead. But the Steelers offense knew just the play to put the game to bed.

On first-and-10 from the Seattle 41, Steelers quarterback Ben Roethlisberger took the snap and pitched the ball to running back Willie Parker, who was running left. Parker then handed the ball to receiver Antwaan Randle El, who was coming on a reverse the other way. Randle El had been a star quarterback in college. He threw a perfect pass to wide receiver Hines Ward in the end zone. The touchdown and extra point put Pittsburgh up by the final score of 21–10.

Randle El wasn't the first non-quarterback to throw a touchdown pass in a Super Bowl. Two running backs had done it in the late 1970s.

Antwaan Randle El winds up to throw his touchdown pass in Super Bowl XL in February 2006.

But both of those passes came from teams that eventually lost. Randle El's toss secured the Steelers' fifth Super Bowl title.

THE PHILLY SPECIAL

Super Bowl LII in February 2018 was one for the record books. The Philadelphia Eagles and New England Patriots piled up offense all night. The teams combined for an NFL-record 1,151 yards. The game featured only one punt. There were many long plays in the shootout. But it was one of the game's shortest plays that defined the game.

With less than one minute remaining in the first half, Philadelphia had a 15–12 lead. The Eagles faced fourth-and-goal at the Patriots 1-yard line. Philadelphia head coach Doug Pederson called timeout to set up the next play.

Quarterback Nick Foles jogged over and said to Pederson, "You want Philly, coach?" Pederson paused for a moment, seemingly stunned. "Yeah, let's do it," he responded.

"Philly" referred to a play the Eagles called "Philly Special." It was a big gamble. When Foles got to the line, he pretended to call an audible. He walked behind his linemen pretending to yell instructions until he was standing where a tight end would normally be. At that moment, center Jason Kelce snapped the ball to running back Corey Clement. Clement then flipped it to tight end Trey Burton, who had jogged into the backfield.

In the meantime, Foles drifted toward the end zone. When Burton got the ball, the confused Patriots defense lost Foles completely. Burton lobbed a pass to the quarterback, who was all alone when he hauled in the score.

Foles was the first quarterback to ever catch a touchdown pass in the Super Bowl. The Eagles took their 22–12 lead into the halftime break. New England eventually came back and made the game close. Philadelphia eventually won 41–33. And while Foles threw the winning touchdown pass with 2:25 left in the fourth quarter, the Philly Special is still the most memorable play from an incredible game.

Nick Foles became the first player to both throw a touchdown pass and catch a touchdown in the same Super Bowl.

CHAPTER FOUR

BEYOND THE GAME

In January 1967, the Green Bay Packers were the champions of the National Football League. The Kansas City Chiefs had won the rival American Football League (AFL). Soon the two leagues would merge. But that year, the two champions met in the first AFL-NFL World Championship Game. Only later would that game be renamed Super Bowl I.

At halftime, two men lined up at opposite 40-yard lines. Each was wearing a jetpack. At the same moment, they shot up into the air. Their "flight" was only about 20 seconds long. The men landed and shook hands.

It was an early look at what the Super Bowl would turn out to be. Today, the game is a huge spectacle full of hype, music,

Jazz trumpeter Al Hirt performed the national anthem before Super Bowl I in January 1967.

and showmanship. The events surrounding the game are sometimes talked about more than the champions.

That was certainly true at Super Bowl III in Miami after the 1968 season. At the time, the AFL was only nine years old. Many fans considered it to be a weaker league. The Packers backed up that opinion by winning the first two Super Bowls easily.

The New York Jets were the AFL champions in 1968. Their quarterback was the good-looking, confident Joe Namath. He was nicknamed "Broadway Joe" for his flashy lifestyle. But few gave Namath's Jets a chance against the NFL-champion Baltimore Colts.

Namath was at a banquet the week of the game. A fan yelled out that the Colts would beat his team easily. Namath shot back, "Hey, I got news for you. We'll win Sunday. I'll guarantee you."

Namath's coach and teammates weren't too happy with his bold claim. But the guarantee captured fans' attention. And when the Jets got off to a solid start, fans couldn't resist the possibility that Namath might actually back up his guarantee. In the end, the Jets did just that. Namath threw for 206 yards. Running back Matt Snell had 121 yards and the team's only touchdown. New York pulled a shocking 16–7 upset.

It was the first year the "Super Bowl" name was used before the game. And Namath's guarantee helped turn the game into a must-see event. More than a half century later, the growth of the Super Bowl owes a lot to his guaranteed win.

Fans hold up a homemade Joe Namath banner at Super Bowl III in January 1969.

THE SHOWER

Many traditions have come from the Super Bowl. Fans witnessed the New York Giants display one of sports' most memorable after Super Bowl XXI in January 1987. It is also certainly the messiest.

With their 39–20 win secured over the Denver Broncos, the Giants continued a celebration they had been doing all season. Two players snuck up behind head coach Bill Parcells holding the team's Gatorade cooler. As the seconds ticked down, they hoisted up the barrel and dumped the sticky sports drink over Parcells's head.

The Gatorade shower soon became a tradition at all levels of football. The Giants weren't the first NFL team to do it. The Chicago Bears had doused coach Mike Ditka after a big regular-season win a few years earlier. But New York did it on football's biggest stage.

GOLDEN VOICE

"The Star-Spangled Banner" has been performed before American sporting events for decades. But in times of crisis, it takes on a bigger meaning. That was true before Super Bowl XXV in January 1991.

Just 10 days before the game, the United States had gone to war in the Middle East. The conflict was on the mind of everyone who was watching. There were 1,700 security officers at Tampa Stadium. A miniature American flag was placed on every seat.

Pop superstar Whitney Houston was set to sing the national anthem. After a jet flyover, Houston stepped onto a stage at midfield. She had actually recorded her version of the anthem two weeks earlier. This is commonly done for big performances to ensure there are no mistakes. Despite singing live into an unplugged microphone, Houston's rendition struck a chord.

A composer had slowed the song's tempo down to bring out the emotion. The singer's amazing voice did the rest. Her soulful version of the song brought many to tears.

The war lasted only a few weeks. But Houston's national anthem has lived on. The song reached No. 20 on the Billboard charts

Whitney Houston was one of the top-selling artists of the 1990s. She also won six Grammy Awards before her death in 2012.

that year. It is still considered one of the greatest renditions of the anthem ever performed.

PURPLE RAIN

The Super Bowl halftime show is one of the top gigs in show business. Music's top stars jump at the chance to perform, even though they aren't paid. Over the years, several music legends have

SWIFT BOWL

Pop star Taylor Swift created a global phenomenon with her "The Eras Tour" that began in 2023. Then she made even more headlines when she began dating Travis Kelce, the popular tight end for the Kansas City Chiefs. When the Chiefs made Super Bowl LVIII, everyone wondered if she'd be there. Swift was, even though she had to race back from a concert in Japan the day before the game. Cameras followed her every reaction to the Chiefs' 25–22 overtime victory over the San Francisco 49ers. The game was watched by a record 123.4 million viewers. Many experts suggested that Swift's enormous popularity brought in many non-football fans.

taken the stage. But none owned it the way Prince did at halftime of Super Bowl XLI in February 2007.

That Prince took the stage at all was a miracle. The game between the Indianapolis Colts and the Chicago Bears was played in a heavy Miami rain. Halftime show organizers worried he might slip on stage or even be electrocuted by a wet wire. They could cancel the show and air the dress rehearsal that had been recorded a few days earlier. But Prince had always taken risks as a performer. He decided to go out anyway. Over the course of his 12-minute set, he defied the conditions and thrilled the crowd with a mix of his own songs and covers of other artists.

The biggest moment was the climax of the show. Prince broke into one of his biggest songs, a 1984 hit called "Purple Rain." As actual rain fell around him, he crushed a long guitar solo. The crowd gave him a huge ovation. After the

In 2024, *Rolling Stone* magazine ranked Prince's performance as the best Super Bowl halftime show of all time.

show was over, one of the men in charge of booking Super Bowl acts said, "How are we ever going to top this?"

BLACKOUT

All was going well for John Harbaugh's Baltimore Ravens in Super Bowl XLVII on February 3, 2013. Early in the third quarter, the Ravens led John's brother Jim Harbaugh's San Francisco 49ers 28–6. Defensive end Arthur Jones sacked San Francisco quarterback Colin Kaepernick to set up a long third-down play. Suddenly, half of the lights in New Orleans's Mercedes-Benz Superdome went dark.

Confusion reigned inside the stadium. The cause of the power outage was a mystery. And no one knew when the lights would come back on. Players wondered if they would be able to finish the game that day. Others feared that the stadium might be under attack. A mysterious man in a dark uniform showed up on the field to ask what the referees planned to do. No one knew who he was.

For 34 minutes, the teams sat on the dark field. The 49ers' locker room didn't have lights, so neither team could leave the field. Finally, stadium workers were able to get the power back on. The 49ers rallied after the strange delay, but Baltimore held on for a 34–31 win. Before the game, the talk had been about how it was the first Super Bowl where the two head coaches were brothers. Afterward, all anyone could talk about was the super blackout.

Ravens coach John Harbaugh, *right*, shares a laugh with linebacker Ray Lewis, *left*, as the team waits for the lights to come back on at the Superdome.

HONORABLE MENTIONS

SUPER BOWL XX JANUARY 26, 1986

Many head coaches have been carried off the field after winning Super Bowls. After Super Bowl XX, the Chicago Bears carried two of them. While some players hoisted head coach Mike Ditka, others scooped up defensive coordinator Buddy Ryan. The team's defensive players loved their coach, who had just led them to a dominant season and was leaving for a head-coaching job with the Philadelphia Eagles.

SUPER BOWL XXIII JANUARY 22, 1989

With time running out, San Francisco's Joe Montana drove his team 92 yards in the final minutes to beat the Cincinnati Bengals. Montana finished the legendary drive by hitting John Taylor on a 10-yard touchdown strike with 32 seconds left. It was the first time since Super Bowl V in January 1971 that the winning score had come in the game's final minute.

SUPER BOWL XXXIV JANUARY 30, 2000

The game was tied 16–16 with two minutes left when St. Louis Rams quarterback Kurt Warner hit receiver Isaac Bruce on a 73-yard game-winning touchdown pass to move ahead of the Tennessee Titans.

Isaac Bruce

U2

SUPER BOWL XXXVI
FEBRUARY 3, 2002

The contest was the first Super Bowl played after the 9/11 terrorist attacks shocked the United States. As part of its halftime show, Irish rock band U2 performed an emotional set in front of a white screen that showed the names of every victim of the attacks.

SUPER BOWL XXXVIII FEBRUARY 1, 2004

The Carolina Panthers had just tied the game late in the fourth quarter when kicker John Kasay booted his kickoff out of bounds. The ensuing penalty meant the New England Patriots got the ball at the 35-yard line. With great field position, Tom Brady drove New England down the field quickly. Adam Vinatieri kicked a game-winning field goal with seconds left.

SUPER BOWL XL FEBRUARY 5, 2006

Popular veteran Pittsburgh Steelers running back Jerome Bettis got a lot of attention leading up to the matchup with the Seattle Seahawks. But early in the third quarter, Bettis's running back partner Willie Parker stole the show. Parker got the ball at the Steelers 25-yard line and burst through the middle. Few Seahawks got near "Fast Willie" as he scampered 75 yards for a score. The play broke the record for longest rush in a Super Bowl by one yard.

GLOSSARY

audible
When the quarterback changes the play at the line of scrimmage after seeing how the defense has lined up.

dynasty
A team that has an extended period of success, usually winning multiple championships in the process.

flat
The area of the field near the line of scrimmage and the sideline.

gaffe
A mistake.

gig
A live performance by a musician.

merge
To join with another to create something new, such as a company, a team, or a league.

momentum
The strength or force that allows something to continue or to grow stronger.

pocket
The area behind the line of scrimmage in which the quarterback is protected by his linemen on passing plays.

scramble
To run around with the ball behind the line of scrimmage while looking for an open receiver.

underdog
The person or team that is not expected to win.

upset
An unexpected victory by a supposedly weaker team or player.

veteran
Having played for many years.

MORE INFORMATION

Books

Graves, Will. *GOATs of Football*. Abdo, 2022.

Hanlon, Luke. *Football Strategies*. Abdo, 2024.

Stathes, Corbu. *Everything Football*. Abdo, 2025.

Online Resources

Booklinks
NONFICTION NETWORK
FREE! ONLINE NONFICTION RESOURCES

To learn more about stunning Super Bowl moments, please visit **abdobooklinks.com** or scan this QR code. These links are routinely monitored and updated to provide the most current information available.

INDEX

About the Author

David J. Clarke is a freelance sportswriter. Originally from Helena, Montana, he now lives in Savannah, Georgia.